BULLY◆PROOFING
Your Child

A Parent's Guide

Carla Garrity, Ph.D.   ◆   Mitchell Baris, Ph.D.
William Porter, Ph.D.

ISBN 1-57035-247-X

Editor: Sharon Green
Text layout and design: Graphics West, Inc.
Cover design: Tracy Katzenberger
Illustrations: Colorado Smiles! Bill Crowley, artist. 719-471-2704

08   8 7

Printed in the United States of America
Published and Distributed by

SOPRIS
WEST™
EDUCATIONAL SERVICES
A Cambium Learning™ Company

4093 Specialty Place ◆ Longmont, Colorado 80504 ◆ 1-800-547-6747
www.sopriswest.com

137BPPT/8-05

ACKNOWLEDGMENTS

I wish to thank Dr. Carla Garrity, without whom the "bully" project would still be only an idea. Many thanks also to the team of professionals who have brought many ideas and experiences to broaden the effort and make more children safe at school and in their community.

William Porter

ABOUT THE AUTHORS

The authors are family and child psychologists working in schools, communities, sports programs, and with families to stop bullying. They enjoy designing creative and individualized programs for parents and children that promote healthy interaction and emotional growth.

This book grew out of requests from parents for greater understanding and strategies for what they could do to bully-proof their children.

CONTENTS

INTRODUCTION

We live in troubled times. There is violence in the lives of our children. As much as we wish for peaceful solutions, our children are exposed to others who use weapons, threats, and bullying.

How do we keep our children safe from bully situations?

There are no magical answers.

The best remedy is to figure out how not to be a victim. Children who have a personal strategy are far less likely to be targeted. Bullying situations are more lethal today than in the past because weapons are in the hands of children. Once a situation is gravely serious, an exit solution is necessary. This runs counter to what we were taught by our own parents. They taught: "Get tough—stand up to the bully." This advice will not serve your children well in the world today. The danger of harm is too great.

Bully-Proofing Your Child will offer you the means to building a comprehensive strategy for your child. You will know:

- ◆ Tools and directions to eliminate the sense of helplessness bullying creates.
- ◆ Ways to direct your efforts in a productive manner for your child's unique personality.
- ◆ Ideas for coping with the fear and trauma.
- ◆ Techniques for teaching your child protective skills.
- ◆ Ways to create caring community, school, and recreational programs that assure safety for your child and others.

PART ONE

UNDERSTANDING THE BULLY/VICTIM PROBLEM

The following chapters will give you an understanding of bully/victim problems. You will learn:

◆ Who is a bully and who is not a bully.

◆ Who is a victim and who is not a victim.

◆ The difference between the ways boys and girls bully.

◆ How bully behavior changes at different ages.

◆ How normal conflict differs from bully/victim problems.

CHAPTER ONE

WHAT IS BULLYING?

In this chapter you will learn that there are two primary types of victims and that some of the old myths about bullies are incorrect.

Bullying happens every seven minutes on elementary school playgrounds. As many girls as boys are the victims. Most of the time no one helps, but surprisingly, another child is more likely to help the victim than an adult.

Bully behavior is real. It hurts and this hurt can last for a long time.

Let's look at how bullying occurs. Not all children get bullied. Most children report that they are teased or called names from time to time, but they bounce back and never become the true victims of bullies. This is important because research has shown that not all children get picked on. Bullies find a certain type of child.

Who Does the Bully Find for a Victim?

Children are at risk to be victims of bullies when they appear vulnerable. Many things can make a child seem this way. Physical characteristics, such as weight, size, handicaps, or coordination problems, can make an individual child stand out. This, however, is not the most important factor. The most important factor that makes a child a victim is that he or she appears anxious, afraid, helpless, and very unlikely to fight back. This emotional vulnerability makes the victim an easy target for the bully to abuse and mistreat.

Two types of children show this emotional vulnerability. One type is called the passive victim and the other is called the provocative victim.

The Passive Victim

These children are shy, insecure and lacking in social skills. Often they play alone at recess time, which makes them easy targets, as no one is nearby to hear or help. They are frequently too fragile to stick up for themselves. Passive victims just give in rather than trying any other alternative. They, honestly, are afraid of the bully and the bully knows that. These children convey their fear through their bodies. Many of them walk with their heads down and their shoulders slumped and make no eye contact. They are easy for the bully to spot and they make prime targets. Special-needs children who have been mainstreamed may fall into this category. Some studies have found that almost five times as many special-needs children are the targets of bullies than their mainstream classmates.

The Provocative Victim

These children are very different from the passive victims. Provocative victims are usually right in the middle of the action on the playground. Often restless and action oriented, they are likely to burst right into the middle of games others are playing. They are rarely alone or quiet. They like interaction and seek it out. Sometimes they push, shove, or use other aggressive tactics to get attention. Nasty remarks burst out of their mouths without thinking. They rarely respect rules or boundaries, wanting to be noticed. Not surprisingly, provocative victims irritate and annoy other children.

At first, you may think a provocative victim sounds like a bully. If you don't look closely, they can appear the same. There are three things, however, that are important in telling the difference between a provocative victim and a true bully.

1. A provocative victim is not purposefully mean or malicious. This type of child is impulsive, but when he or she realizes that another child has been hurt, feels badly and will apologize.

The provocative victim is like a child who acts without thinking but doesn't mean to hurt another.

2. A provocative victim typically loses to the bully. This type of child is not as quick witted, mean spirited, and as cunning as the bully. The bully will overpower this child and win.

3. A bully has friends; a provocative victim tends not to.

Why would a bully pick on a provocative victim? There are many answers. One is that the provocative victim irritates others and the bully wants to show who is boss. A bully can justify picking on a child who is irritating. Picking on a provocative victim creates a lot of attention on the playground. Unlike the passive victim, who cries and trembles, the provocative victim fights back with a great deal of gusto and noise. This attracts attention. Other children come running over to see what the commotion is all about. Soon a crowd has gathered to watch. This satisfies the bully's need for power and domination.

Bullies like having power and often will come back to prey on the same victims, passive or provocative, time and time again. An unfortunate situation develops on the playground when this happens. Other children begin to gather and watch; some actually experience excitement from the drama and action. This may seem hard to believe but it is little different from the excitement adults derive when watching violence in movies, on television, or on the nightly news. Bullying is exciting news on the childhood playground scene. Being part of the action may even be appealing, and other children may decide to join in. A contagion effect begins to happen. Soon the bully has far more children on his or her side and the victim feels even more helpless. When a scene such as this plays itself out day after day, the victimized child grows more miserable, desperate, and incapable of handling the situation. If the cycle has grown this serious, it will not turn itself around without adult help.

Who Are the Bullies?

Most people have an image of a bully: A bully is usually a boy, physically large, a poor student, and basically insecure. All of these are completely false. Bullies are not all boys; girls are bullies as well. Bullies are typically average students and are not failing school. Low self-esteem is not a problem for a bully. In fact, most bullies have an inflated image of themselves. They enjoy the power that aggression brings and they feel entitled to recognition, privilege, and special treatment. It is personality style, not size or gender, that defines a bully.

A typical bully is a child who:

- Values power and the rewards that aggression can bring.
- Lacks compassion and empathy for others.
- Lacks guilt for his or her actions.
- Sincerely believes that it is okay to treat others in a cruel fashion.
- Likes to dominate and be in charge.
- Thinks it is okay to be abusive in order to get whatever he or she wants.
- Avoids adults and plays out of the sight of adult eyes.
- Is verbally convincing.
- Projects problems onto others.

As a parent, you must appraise your child honestly. As difficult as it may be to admit, your child may be the bully claiming to be a victim in order to avoid responsibility for his or her behavior. Bullies are capable of manipulating their parents into believing that the problem is the other person's fault.

Try the following question with your child:

"Do others sometimes pick on you?"

If the answer is "Nobody picks on me," you may have a child who is a bully. Bullies will not admit to even occasional run-ins with other kids.

Now try a second question:

"How do you feel when you see someone else getting picked on?"

If the answer is "He probably got what he deserved," then you must look further into your child's behavior. Most children feel badly when they see another child being picked on, even though they may not be brave enough to do anything or to confront the bully. Children who lack this feeling for others are at risk for doing emotional or physical harm because they cannot relate to the feelings another child experiences.

The outcome in life is very poor for children who are bullies. These children are three times more likely to have committed a crime by early adulthood. They are less likely to finish college, maintain a job, or establish a good marriage. Girls who bully are more likely to raise children who will bully. None of this needs to happen. Bullies as well as victims can have the opportunity to be productive and happy adults if their personalities are recognized early in childhood and redirected. The rest of the book will help you in rating your own child and redirecting him or her to a healthy pathway.

CHAPTER TWO

HOW BOYS BULLY AND HOW GIRLS BULLY

Boys are not the only ones who bully. Girls bully too, but they are harder to spot. Unless someone watches closely, they will not see bullying between girls. While boys are more likely to use or threaten physical aggression, girls are sneaky. They use gossiping, whispering threats, and spreading rumors to hurt others. The abuse is more emotional than physical but girls report that it hurts just as much, if not more, than being hit.

Bullying Behavior

Look at Table 1: **Bullying Behaviors Chart**. There are four different styles of bullying. Girls use **Social Alienation and Intimidation**. Boys use **Physical or Verbal Aggression**. Notice that there is a scale across the top ranging from Mild to Severe. Children are different in how much they can

TABLE 1 Bullying Behaviors Chart

MILD	MODERATE	SEVERE
PHYSICAL AGGRESSION		
◆ Pushing ◆ Shoving ◆ Spitting	◆ Kicking ◆ Hitting	◆ Defacing property ◆ Stealing	◆ Physical acts that are demeaning and humiliating, but not bodily harmful (e.g., de-panting) ◆ Locking in a closed or confined space	◆ Physical violence against family or friends	◆ Threatening with a weapon ◆ Inflicting bodily harm
SOCIAL ALIENATION		
◆ Gossiping ◆ Embarrassing	◆ Setting up to look foolish ◆ Spreading rumors about	◆ Ethnic slurs ◆ Setting up to take the blame	◆ Publicly humiliating (e.g., revealing personal information) ◆ Excluding from group ◆ Social rejection	◆ Maliciously excluding ◆ Manipulating social order to achieve rejection ◆ Malicious rumormongering	◆ Threatening with total isolation by peer group
VERBAL AGGRESSION		
◆ Mocking ◆ Name calling ◆ Dirty looks ◆ Taunting	◆ Teasing about clothing or possessions	◆ Teasing about appearance	◆ Intimidating telephone calls	◆ Verbal threats of aggression against property or possessions	◆ Verbal threats of violence or of inflicting bodily harm
INTIMIDATION		
◆ Threatening to reveal personal information ◆ Graffiti ◆ Publicly challenging to do something	◆ Defacing property or clothing ◆ Playing a dirty trick	◆ Taking possessions (e.g., lunch, clothing, toys)	◆ Extortion ◆ Sexual/racial taunting	◆ Threats of using coercion against family or friends	◆ Coercion ◆ Threatening with a weapon

take. Some children get very upset with mild bullying. These children usually are those who:

- Are alone, shy, or lonely.
- Have a learning disability and cannot quickly process social cues.
- Have been bullied in the past.
- Have suffered a trauma such as a death, divorce, or other loss.
- Are physically weak and cannot defend themselves.

Girl Bullying

Girls usually start bullying by first or second grade. At this age, they typically use put-downs. One girl, or a group of girls, will walk up to a victim and tell her that her hair is an ugly color or that her clothes are stupid looking. The put-downs are usually about clothing, hair, or overall appearance. By third to fourth grade, the tactics change. Girls start to leave out the victim. They form cliques or groups and stand together, taunting or harassing the victim. This is often done at recess or lunchtime but not

Put-downs

Girls Use Words to Bully

Networking or Group Bullying

Social Alienation

Gossiping

in so obvious a way that the adults notice. Some girls take it a step further and promise that the excluded girl can be part of their group if she does something for them. This may be bringing them money or food. It could also include something humiliating or embarrassing they ask her to do. Many victims believe this will truly buy them a chance to be "in," and they do what is asked only to find the bullying does not stop. By fifth to sixth grade, the situation grows more serious. A victimized girl may find she is receiving intimidating or threatening notes that warn her that something bad will happen. Gossiping and spreading very damaging and embarrassing stories are commonplace.

Boy Bullying

Boys do not truly change their tactics as they grow older. Throughout childhood, boys bully with physical aggression or by threatening to use physical aggression. Bullying is a quick jab, push or shove, elbow or knee, or head thrust into a wall or locker. Whatever it is, it hurts. It also is quick and over before anyone sees what is happening. The bully's size or strength is intimidating. Boys bully by creating fear and an always present threat of harm from physical abuse. Boys see bullies as large, strong, and

**Threats of
Aggression**

"Forget it,
I'm going to
kill you."

"Please don't
kill me."

powerful. The drawing of a bully by a boy shows a bully who is intimidating physically because of his size or strength.

How Bullies Find Their Victims

It is fairly easy for a bully to find a victim. Recall that bullies are impulsive with a strong need to dominate others. They like having power. Finding someone who will not fight back, who is alone, or lacking in social skills, is an easy way for the bully to feel very powerful. Picking on a competent child with a circle of friends is far harder. The bully might not come away the winner. Looking foolish is not something the bully will risk. Finding a sure and easy target is the best way for a bully to let others know that he or she is in charge.

CHAPTER THREE

IS IT BULLYING OR NORMAL CONFLICT?

Many parents worry that their children are victims. Most children complain from time to time about harassment and teasing from others. Anger and hurtful remarks are part of conflict at all ages. It is important to know how children of different ages play together. Bully/victim problems become more serious and change as children grow older.

In this chapter you will learn how to tell the difference between true bully/victim problems and normal conflict between children. **Sometimes** it is just normal peer conflict and sometimes it is the beginning of a true bully problem. There are three basic ways to know if your child is truly being bullied:

1. The bully picks on your child day after day. It never seems to let up.

2. The bully wins because your child is smaller, younger, or less socially able to cope.

3. Your child is afraid and very upset. The bully sees it all as "no big deal" or as "deserved." The bully actually enjoys making your child upset.

Why such meanness? How can we fortify our children against this? There are no simple answers. Conflict between children who interact together is inevitable. It is part of learning how to have relationships— how to share, compromise, and work together cooperatively. This does not just come naturally. Children go through stages of social development. How they handle their differences changes as they grow older. Parents who under-stand this sequence can help teach at these moments of conflict during normal play. Research shows that children who have good role models for problem-solving are far less likely to be either a victim or a bully.

Ages 3 to 5

Preschoolers play beside each other but not in a give-and-take fashion. Watch two three-year olds with a box of building blocks. They will most likely each be building their own structure but with one pile of shared blocks. Play will go happily until one of them takes the last block or takes the block the other one needs or wants. The child who lost out will most likely grab the block or begin yelling loudly. Asking, sharing, or compro-mising are not possibilities the three-year old even knows about.

What Can a Parent Do?

Give a clear message that hurting others is not okay.

> State that there are consequences of biting, hitting, throwing, or hurt-ing a friend.
>
> Offer a fair solution. For example, say "Hitting will not get you a turn on the tricycle. After (name) rides around the playground one time, then it will be your turn."
>
> Help put it into action.

Ages 5 and 6

Kids still fight over toys and possessions but now they add verbal insults and put-downs. They want their own way, to have the first turn, or to play with the toy as long as they want. If they don't win, they threaten, they tattle, and then they act mean. By this age, children have figured out that they are more likely to win if an adult does not see what they are do-ing. Few feel guilty for long, but the feeling is beginning at this age. Seeing another child's pain and responding to it is a positive sign. The child who shows no awareness of another's feelings may be on the road to becoming a bully. The child who gives up, gives in, and tattles but never sticks up for his or her rights may be on the road to being a victim.

What Can a Parent Do?

Teach social skills—don't whine, demand, or retreat.

> Teach how to approach others. Look for someone alone or a group of three or more children. Just go join them. A group of two children playing together is the hardest group to join.
>
> Build ideas for how to ask for needs to be met.
>
> Point out the pain caused to the other child. For example, say "You go first this time but I get to go first next time." or "Please, may I have the swing when you're done."
>
> Connect the actions and consequences—"He is crying because you pushed him off the trike and took it."
>
> State what is okay to do.
>
> Offer a solution and stay close by to see that it is followed—"You get the trike for twice around the driveway, then [other child] gets a turn. Tomorrow [other child] goes first."

Ages 6 to 8

This is the age of games and sports with rules. Self-control is being learned and rules help to enforce the concepts of fairness, taking turns, and sharing. The world, however, is still black and white to a six-year old. Either you broke the rule or you didn't; there is no gray. Children take one side or the other; it is either right or it is wrong.

Being good at something is terribly important at this age. Sports and athletics are where most children spend their free time. Parents who have unathletic children need to work to find other outlets with similar children. Teasing over being inferior is so commonplace that it is almost an invitation to ridicule to place a child in an activity he or she cannot master. Power is important in the six- to eight-year-old peer group, and kids vie for it. Size, strength, and agility will typically assure a boy of a power position in his peer culture. Girls win power through social connections. Putting down a girl and excluding her for her clothing or looks is all too common. The girl delivering the put- down often gains prestige and position in the peer group and takes one more rival out of the loop. Tattling,

19

distorting the truth, and gossiping are all part of the playground culture of six- to eight-year-old girls. Sadly, assuring this status in the peer group takes precedence for some children over and above protecting another from the hurt of rejection. Group affiliation is the hallmark of middle childhood. Differences are a disadvantage and similarities are emphasized.

What Can a Parent Do?

Parents need to listen during the carpool drive to school, at sporting events, and at parties. Opportunities to teach character development are plentiful at this age. The problem-solving skills taught at this age set a foundation for life. Take time to talk and teach your child about:

Acceptance of diversity.

Rejection in a kind way.

Refusing to exclude another child.

Developing compassion and empathy.

Awareness of others' feelings.

Finding an outcome that benefits everyone.

Not bullying back, but sticking up for himself or herself.

Ages 9 and Up

The world rapidly shifts to gray for children over age nine. Problems no longer have simple black and white solutions. Complexities creep in, value judgments are made, and issues or morals and justice matter. Children worry about "what is fair." This is when compromise begins, which is sacrificing something for the good of the team or the relationship. This is not turn-taking—"You first today and me tomorrow and everything will be even." Compromise is: "I give up some of what I want and you give up some of what you want so we can reach a goal and preserve our relationship." The message is that the relationship matters as much or more than individual needs and wants.

This takes maturity. A child must know and recognize his or her own feelings, have empathy for the feelings of others, and be able to regulate strong emotions. These are the building blocks for relationships in jobs and families later in life. Bullies usually do not master these steps. Victims, on the other hand, are so eager for a relationship that they sacrifice themselves in the process. Neither is healthy. Teach your child a balance between looking out for his or her needs yet respecting those of others.

What Can a Parent Do?

Talk and talk some more about the complexities of compromise.

> Take real-life examples such as a call a coach made that seemed doubtful, information out of the daily news, or court cases and discuss the viewpoint of both sides.
>
> Model good problem-solving in your own life.

The following table (Table 2) summarizes the typical conflicts at each age and possible resolutions.

TABLE 2   Conflict and Resolution

Age	Typical Conflict	Preferred Styles of Resolution
3–5 years	Conflict likely over toys, possessions ("It's mine"), or going first	Action oriented Separate the children Change the topic No-nonsense, direct and concise
5–6 years	Selfishness, wanting own way Threatening with tattling or not playing again ("I'm not inviting you to my birthday.")	Connect actions and consequences Undo what the offender did No-nonsense or problem-solving
6–8 years	What's fair and what isn't Teasing, gossiping, feeling superior Putting down, accusing of something not true or distorted	Mutual negotiation with help Understanding of others' intentions Problem-solving
9 years and up	Bossiness, tattling, put-downs, showing off, betrayal	Build empathy Talking things out Negotiating Compromising

Remember that normal peer conflict is not bullying. Know the difference. Typically, peers in conflict are on equal footing. They have a relationship with each other and the primary goal is not one of hurting the other.

Conflicts are part of life. Teach your child how to recognize and solve typical problems with peers. Also teach your child how to recognizing bullying and know quickly that bullying is not normal, fair, or a conflict that can be solved. It is conflict to get away from. A bully doesn't want to solve a problem; a bully wants to hurt, humiliate, and control in order to feel powerful. Bullying is not something to tolerate.

Use Table 3 to help your child recognize the difference.

TABLE 3   Recognizing the Difference

Normal Peer Conflict	Bullying
Equal power between friends	Imbalance of power between friends
Individuals often play together	Individuals rarely play together
Happens occasionally	Repeated negative actions
Accidental	Purposeful
Not serious	Serious with threat of physical or emotional harm
Equal emotional reactions	Strong emotional reaction from victim and little or no emotional reaction from bully
Not seeking power or attention	Seeking power, control, or material things
Not trying to get something	Attempt to gain material things or power
Remorse—will take responsibility	No remorse—blame victim
Effort to solve the problem	No effort to solve the problem

PART TWO

SOLVING BULLY/VICTIM PROBLEMS

The following chapters will give you a step-by-step program for helping your children feel empowered to protect themselves as well as for building their self-esteem in social, school, sports, and recreational activities.

Ideas will be given for:

- ◆ Helping your child build a protective shield.
- ◆ Mobilizing the community to stand up against bullying.
- ◆ Using the power of the peer group to change the climate to a safe and caring one.
- ◆ Intervening at school.
- ◆ Implementing strategies in sports and recreational programs.
- ◆ Handling friends and peer pressure.
- ◆ Building skills for life.

CHAPTER FOUR

HOW TO RATE YOUR OWN CHILD

Recall the **Bullying Behaviors Chart** (Table 1) from Chapter 2. Bullying comes in many different forms. There are physical aggression and verbal abuse, intimidation, and social alienation. The way children experience bullying varies. Some can tolerate moderate bullying without feeling done in; others feel very upset when just called a name. Each child deserves to be respected and not to be told "get over it." As a parent, you want to rate your own child's likelihood to be picked on by a bully. Identifying traits in your child as early as possible will help. Some traits can be changed if you begin early. Others are the "luck of the draw" and may not be as open to change. Nevertheless, you can still help by giving your child coping strategies and by playing your part in creating a climate where children feel safe. No child needs to be a defenseless victim of a bully.

Recognizing Your Child's Reactions

Two types of victims were described earlier: passive victims and provocative victims. **Passive victims** are the ones who don't fight back or stick up for themselves. They give in because they lack the temperament and/or social skills to defend themselves. After trying meekly, they hide out of fear and anxiety. These children are not fun for others to play with, so they end up alone. Bullies find them easy to pick on because they don't know how to protect themselves. As you look at the scale below, the passive victims fall toward the **underreactive** end of the scale.

Provocative victims are at the opposite end of the same scale. These children are restless, irritable, and will fight back. They provoke, tease, and "egg on" the bully. Yet they lose and usually end up ridiculed. Their problem is **overreactivity**. They leap right into new experiences without thinking. They also wear parents to exhaustion with their activity level and "accident proneness."

Knowing your child and rating him or her along the continuum below will guide you in which behaviors need reshaping to avoid bullying.

Rate your child's reactivity on the scale below:

◆ The underreactive child is at risk of becoming a passive victim.

| |_____|_____|_____|_____|_____|_____| |

Underreactive   **Overreactive**
likely to be dominated,   likely to pick
pushed around, taken   unnecessary
advantage of   battles

◆ The overreactive child is at risk of becoming a provocative victim.

Most parents know from early childhood which tendency their child is exhibiting. If you feel uncertain, complete the following checklist. Look at where your checks are. If they are nearer the right-hand side of the scale, you probably have an overreactive or provocative child. If they are nearer the left-hand side of the scale, your child is more likely to be underreactive and at risk to be a passive victim. If they are in the middle, or "sometimes" column, your child is most likely not at high risk to be bullied.

NO	SOMETIMES	YES
	Adventure seeking	

| |_____|_____|_____|_____|_____|_____| |

NO	SOMETIMES	YES

Enjoys unexpected stimulation such as fireworks,
a popping balloon, or the circus

Enjoys new activities such as riding a bike, skating, or a sports event

Loves novelty and new situations, places, and friends

Friends come and go—long-term relationships are not built

Likes to roughhouse

Shaping Your Child's Natural Temperament

Children who are not at either end of the continuum are the least likely to be picked on by bullies. These children are resilient. They roll with the punches and shift gears as need be. Although you cannot change the natural disposition of your child, a parent can do a great deal to shape a child's reactivity.

Now that you have rated your child, you know if you have an underreactive or overreactive child. You will benefit your child by helping shape his or her behaviors away from the extremes. Try these ideas.

Underreactive children benefit from:

◆ Modeling and encouragement to express feelings.

◆ Gradual exposure to new experiences.

◆ Support—but not overprotectiveness—during difficult times to help meet the challenges.

- Learning skills to manage anxiety.
- Social skills training—what to say and how to say it.
- Being allowed to experience some of life's difficulties and hard moments.

Overreactive children benefit from:

- Learning self-regulation skills—for example "stop and think."
- Having the consequences of their own behavior pointed out clearly and firmly.
- Being expected to have compassion and empathy for others.
- Learning to see themselves as others see them.
- Earning freedom and privileges.
- Participating in cooperative group activities.
- Guidance and discussion rather than punishment without explanation.
- Direction and help in learning specific skills for getting their needs met appropriately.
- Learning to express emotions, especially anger, in a regulated manner.
- Being expected to do thoughtful things for others.

Life events and circumstances also further shape or entrench a child's basic tendency. These external events may not be something you can prevent or change. However, you can identify them as high risk factors and help your child in developing ideas for ways to manage and cope. Some high risk factors are:

- Lack of athletic skill
- Attention deficit disorder
- Hyperactivity
- Extreme giftedness
- Learning disability
- Past trauma
- Shyness
- Physical weakness
- Small size in a boy

Children who do best in life are resilient, optimistic, and good social-problem solvers. These things can be taught. The rest of this book will show you how to do this for your child.

Think for a moment, before you leave this chapter: what are your child's triggers or buttons? These are the comments others make that arouse a strong emotional response in your child. This might be teasing about size or lack of athletic ability. These might include insults about family, appearance, or skills.

Here are some common buttons for many children:

- ◆ Size—big, small, fat, thin
- ◆ Appearance—large nose, big feet, curly hair
- ◆ Personality—overly sensitive
- ◆ Family—heritage
- ◆ School performance—good or bad
- ◆ Athletic ability

Buttons are typically specific to a child's vulnerabilities. Once you and your child have identified these buttons, the next chapters will guide you toward developing skills to protect these buttons. Use the figure on the next page to write in your child's personal buttons.

CHAPTER FIVE

GIVING YOUR CHILD A PROTECTIVE SHIELD

A protective shield is a child's armor. Every child needs one to feel safe and to feel okay when picked on. A protective shield is something you put on when you feel threatened, just as you put on a raincoat when it rains. You carry it with you at all times and pull it out when needed.

There are six protective strategies; all are effective and easy to use. All children can learn them. Imagining them on a shield helps children to remember. When you feel scared, it's difficult to think. The shield makes it easy to remember the "safe" words.

HA HA SO is an easy way to remember the six things to try when a bully comes along. They stand for:

H - Help	H - Humor	S - Self Talk
A - Assert Yourself	A - Avoid	O - Own It

Help means knowing when and how to get help. It also means knowing who will help. Talk to your child about who the adults and children are who can be counted on.

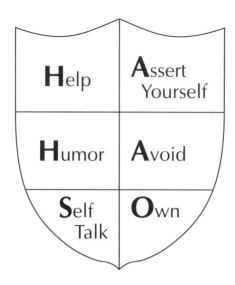

Assert Yourself means learning when to stand up to a bully and when not to. To use this strategy, the victim looks the bully in the eye and says, "I don't like you telling untrue stories about me. What you are doing is mean. Stop doing it." This strategy should not be used in instances of severe bullying or when the victim could be hurt.

Humor means turning a difficult situation into a funny one. This is a surprise tactic, which usually catches the bully off guard. Other kids will laugh and the bully gets defused. This is a difficult strategy for a frightened child. Thinking on your feet, especially thinking of something funny, is not easy when you feel afraid. Getting ideas from stories, parents, movies, and any other resource helps. Practicing good comebacks also helps. Don't use tactics that put down the bully because this will make matters worse. The idea is to change the situation from a power play to a funny situation.

Avoid means knowing how and when to walk away. This is the strategy most children use. Some go to enormous lengths to avoid running into the bully. Disengagement is one form of avoidance, but a more difficult one than just staying out of the bully's reach. Disengagement is walking away while leaving an assertive message that you are not interested in engaging in conflict. It takes courage and practice but it is well worth it. The necessary skills are discussed in the next chapter.

Self Talk   is a way to continue to feel good about yourself when someone else is putting you down. Children imagine putting on a tape or CD in their heads that plays good thoughts and positive messages. You can help your child by working to develop these positive statements.

Own It   means agreeing with the put-down in order to make light of it. It means developing the capacity to laugh at oneself. This strategy is easy to use and very effective because the bully does not expect it. It is best used when being teased or made fun of about something such as clothing or hairstyle. "I agree with you. This shirt is the ugliest color I've ever seen. Glad you think so too," might be an "own it" comeback. If, on the other hand, your child is being put down about something inherent to his identity or person, such as ethnicity, religion, or disability, this tactic is not a good idea because it could lower the self-esteem of the victim.

Learning the right strategy for the situation takes time and practice. Sometimes the first thing tried does not work. This is why there are six strategies, and an easy way to remember all six is with the **HA HA SO** acronym. Help your child put on his or her protective shield by practicing each strategy. Just like a pilot practices emergency procedures, children also must practice to be ready for a real "emergency" or bully situation. Like a pilot, your child will think more clearly and react with his or her best effort if there have been practice sessions.

The next chapter teaches you how to build even more protective skills, depending on whether your child is overreactive or underreactive. The end of Chapter 6 presents situations you can use to practice these protective skills.

CHAPTER SIX

TAILOR-MAKING A SHIELD

If you have an underreactive or overreactive child, building a tailor-made shield will give your child extra protection against bullies. At least three steps are involved in custom-making a protective shield. Your child must first learn what to ignore, what to respond to, and when it is best to walk away. If a child chooses to respond, the best response is one of assertion that is neither too aggressive nor too passive. These skills are taught in this chapter.

Step 1. Evaluate the Situation

Encourage your child, when faced by a bully, to think first. Decide if this is a battle worth fighting or one that is best handled by walking away. Teach your child to choose his or her battles and to have the skills available to elect to walk away and disengage. Assess the advantages of both taking a stand and walking away. The use of the protective shield in combination with disengagement is a very powerful tool.

Many problems are solved just by walking away. It takes two to fight, and choosing to leave a fight is sometimes the best strategy. It may come as a surprise to learn this is the most difficult strategy for children to learn.

Most children want to fight back or to get the last word in. They think that if they walk away, they have not won. Even shy children, who walk away, tend to do it without assertiveness and determination. Choosing not to fight does not mean meekly giving in. It means taking away the power of the bully by refusing to engage with him or her. The bully wants a reaction. Bullies feel powerful when they see the pain and suffering of the victim. By not showing pain and suffering, by walking away in an assertive manner, the bully's bluff has been called. Choosing not to fight can be a winning strategy when it is done effectively and the victim takes control. The biggest winners are those who are not on the scene when violence escalates.

Table 4 lists some general guidelines you can use to teach your child when to take a stand and when to choose to let it go.

TABLE 4   General Tips for Evaluating a Situation

Take a Stand	Let It Go
Threats of physical or sexual assault	Threats that are more pat phrases, idioms, or figures of speech than real threats
Strong derogatory remarks about race, ethnicity, or family that are constant, intense, or repetitive	Occasional racial remarks or ethnic put-downs that are primarily insensitive, not cruel. Education may be a better remedy than escalation.
Extortion of large amounts of money	Small amounts demanded and there is no giving back
Relationship that is important and/or there is caring for the other person	No relationship, and no interest in building one
A bully showing some capacity for compassion, empathy, and mutuality	A child who can both give and take. Offer once to share, state what you expect in return, and see what happens
Bullying behavior which is increasing in magnitude and intensity	Bullying behavior which is constant but there are no signs of escalation

Step 2. Define the Line between Taking a Stand and Letting It Go

Help your child define where his or her limits lie.

Look at the line below. It is the same line you saw in Chapter 5. Where did your child fall on the line?

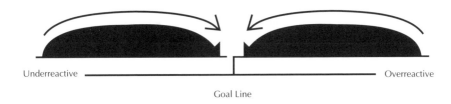

Underreactive ———————————————— Overreactive

Goal Line

The goal is to shape toward the middle. Effective children size up a situation and decide quickly what to do. They are not bound by their tendency to be overreactive or underreactive. They have the personal strength to make a choice. They also have the skills to put their choice into action.

If you have an underreactive child, your goal is to teach how not to be taken advantage of. If you have an overreactive child, your goal is to teach what is worth reacting to and not to fight back every time someone or something provokes him or her.

Step 3. Moving toward the Middle

The most effective protective shield is one that gives your child his or her **own power of choice**. Children who do not become victims don't overdo and don't "underdo." These children learn not to be taken advantage of but also not to react to every slight, taunt, threat, or put-down.

Learning to disengage effectively is one of the most important skills you can teach your child. Disengagement means making an assertive statement with self-confidence and then walking away. A child who says nothing and slinks away, eyes on the ground and shoulders slumped, is not skilled at disengagement. The bully takes one look and knows he or she has won. The body language says, "I'm terrified and too afraid to say or do anything." An underreactive child must practice the walk, the style, and the presentation of disengagement. Take a stand, say a few simple

37

words, shoulders up, head high, and then walk away are the skills needed as the victim puts on the custom-made protective shield. Think like a knight in armor.

What can you teach your child to say? Here are some examples:

"I don't get into those kinds of fights."

"I'll share today. Next time, I expect you to share."

"What you just said isn't worth my time."

These statements have just the right amount of reaction. They establish the line down the middle—the goal line.

Remember, there are three steps involved in disengagement:

1. Make one statement while standing firmly.

2. Announce your intention to disengage from the situation.

3. Then do it with pride and conviction.

If your child is underreactive, the walking away part will be easy but the statement or gesture will be very challenging. The manner of walking will also be difficult to master. Practice and practice with your child. Use Table 5: **Skills to Disengage for the Underreactive Child**.

TABLE 5   Skills to Disengage for the Underreactive Child

1. Make a statement or gesture that says you intend to ignore what was said or done to you.

    "I don't get into fights over things like that."

    "You are welcome to your opinion."

    "I'll share today. Next time, I expect you to share."

2. Walk away.

3. Think something positive to yourself as you walk away in a self-confident manner (positive self-talk).

    Think of something you are good at doing.

    Think of the best time you had on vacation.

    Remember your family, friends, pets—the ones who care about you.

TABLE 5   (*continued*)

4. Find someone to be with. Don't just walk away; walk toward a teacher, friend, parent, or other accepting social situation.

5. Get another person's perspective on what happened. Talk to someone you trust (parent, friend, teacher, etc.). Ask that person whether the words or action seemed hurtful.

If your child is overreactive, the withdrawal and walking away will be the most difficult. You will also have to practice. Use Table 6: **Skills to Disengage for the Overreactive Child**.

TABLE 6   Skills to Disengage for the Overreactive Child

1. Think about what gets to you.

   Before you are in a bully/victim situation, identify your own buttons.

2. If someone pushes one of your buttons, stay calm. Try these things:

   Say your multiplication tables in your head.

   Count backward from 30 to 1.

   Think about the last time you were really bored.

3. Do **not** continue to think about what the other person did or said to you.

   If you respond, you are handing control over to the bully.

   Doing nothing means that you win!

   The other person lost because you stayed in control.

   Now, plan for the next time this same person tries to get to you. Remember that there will be a next time. People who like to push the buttons of others usually try, try again. The second and third times might be worse. If you manage to resist overreacting, by the third time they usually find someone else to pick on. When it happens again, remind yourself of these things:

   It gets worse before it gets better.

   Winning is **not** who is best at put-downs.

   Winning is taking care of your own emotions.

Remind your child that bullies like power struggles. They are not likely to change or stop the first time a victim tries on his or her custom-made shield. It will take time.

The next chapter presents some bully/victim scenarios for practice. Read these together with your child and then create some of your own.

CHAPTER SEVEN

PRACTICE SCENARIOS USING THE SHIELD

The following pages present some sample bully scenarios. See what solutions you and your child can arrive at together. Some suggested ideas for you to compare with your strategies follow each scenario.

Practice Scenarios

Use these three steps as you practice the following scenarios.

1. Review **HA HA SO**.
   Put on your protective shield.

2. Choose which strategy will work best.
   Assert yourself.

3. Review **Skills to Disengage** (Tables 5 and 6).
   Choose to walk away.

> **Feel Proud.**
> **You have successfully protected yourself.**

S C E N A R I O   1
Has this ever happened to you?

 You are playing ball with a friend.

A bully walks over, picks up the ball, and heaves it across the playground.

You are mad. What would you do?

S C E N A R I O   1

	Underreactive	Overreactive
TRY THIS FIRST	Say, "Thanks. That end of the field is a better place to play." (**H**UMOR) or Say, "I wish I could throw like you." (**O**WN IT) or Say, "Would you teach us to throw like that?" (**A**SSERT YOURSELF)	Ignore him and go get your ball. (**A**VOID)
TRY THIS NEXT	Say, "You sure must feel tough to be taking a ball from somebody younger." (**A**SSERT YOURSELF)	Quit playing ball and go do something else. (**A**VOID)

IMPORTANT

Remember:
I'm not going to let him see
me cry or get mad.
I'll think of the thing I like
about myself.
(**S**ELF-TALK)

SCENARIO 2
Has this ever happened to you?

 Your mom packed a really nice treat in your lunch.

A bully comes over and says, "Oh, what do you have in there for me?" He opens your lunch and takes your special treat.

You want it back, but you are scared. What would you do?

S C E N A R I O 2

	Underreactive	Overreactive
TRY THIS FIRST	Say loudly, "Tom is really hungry today. Anybody else have some treats for Tom?" (GET **H**ELP, **H**UMOR)	Say, "You may have some of that but you can't take it all." (**O**WNING AND JOINING)
TRY THIS NEXT	Say, "Sure you can have it. Hope you like hot sauce." (**H**UMOR)	Say, "That's fine today, but I'll expect you to share your treat next time." (**A**SSERT YOURSELF)

IMPORTANT

Remember:
Say to yourself:
"I won't let him see me beg, whine, or cry. I will think of what makes me a strong and likable person."
(**S**ELF-TALK)

S C E N A R I O 3
Has this ever happened to you?

 You are walking into school wearing something new, like new boots on a rainy day.

Somebody behind you says, "Look at those duck feet. Ha, ha, ha."

You wish you could disappear. What do you say?

SCENARIO 3

	Underreactive	Overreactive
TRY THIS FIRST	Say, "Thanks for noticing. I'm glad you like them." (**A**SSERT YOURSELF, **H**UMOR)	Ignore the remark and keep walking. (**A**VOID)
TRY THIS NEXT	Say, "Yeah. They are funny, aren't they?" and laugh, too. (**O**WNING IT)	Say, "I'll leave them to you when I outgrow them." (**H**UMOR)

IMPORTANT

Remember:
Think of something you like
about yourself.
(**S**ELF-TALK)

SCENARIO 4
Has this ever happened to you?

 You go out to recess. The kids are playing Red Rover.

You ask which side you can play on, and they tell you, "Nobody else can play." A few minutes later, you see somebody else go over and join the game.

You feel sad. You wish you could be included. What can you do?

S C E N A R I O   4

	Underreactive	Overreactive
TRY THIS FIRST	Don't ask again if you can play, just join in. (**O**WNING, JOINING)	Look around for someone else to play with. (**A**VOID)
TRY THIS NEXT	Go stand in the line by someone you are sure likes you. If someone says, "You can't play," respond with, "Sure I can." (**A**SSERT YOURSELF)	Look around for enough kids to start another game. (GET **H**ELP)

IMPORTANT

Remember:
"No, you can't play," means
"TRY AGAIN LATER."
(**S**ELF-TALK)

SCENARIO 5
Has this ever happened to you?

 You are tall for your age.

At your last school, everyone thought that was neat.

You change schools. At your new school, the children say things like:

"How's the weather up there?"
"Hey, Bean Pole."
"There goes the Jolly Green Giant."

You hate it when they tease you like this. What can you do?

SCENARIO 5

	Underreactive	Overreactive
TRY THIS FIRST	Say, "I plan to play basketball and make a million on a pro team." (**A**SSERT YOURSELF, **H**UMOR)	Say, "How are the grass blades down there? Do they need water?" (**H**UMOR)
TRY THIS NEXT	Say, "I like being tall. Thanks for noticing." (**O**WN IT)	Say, "I can think of something about you that would hurt your feelings. I don't like to treat people like that." Then walk away. (**A**SSERT YOURSELF, **A**VOID)

IMPORTANT

Remember:
Think about the things you
like about yourself.
(SELF-TALK)

CHAPTER EIGHT

DECIDING WHETHER TO CHANGE SCHOOLS

More than 20% of children say they are frightened through much of the school day. Many avoid the bathroom, lunchroom, and even recess because these are the places where most bullying occurs.

Parents do not know what or how much to believe of what they hear from their children, who to approach at the school, or how to approach them. Furthermore they are left with the dilemma of what to do if the school is not responsive to their concerns.

Yet most children don't tell anyone about their fears. They report that no one helps them anyway and the bully will retaliate. Parents are appalled when they hear this. They consider school to be a place where children can find help if they need it. Unfortunately, this is not the case. Many schools are installing metal detectors and most schools have a weapons policy. These safeguards do not always help nor can they stop the fear and intimidation a bully instills. Teachers cannot be there at every moment. And bullies are clever. They can create a sense of fear in a matter of seconds without teachers or staff ever suspecting what is happening.

Changing the School Environment

The real key to solving bully/victim problems within the school is changing the climate of the school to one in which the silent bystander children are mobilized into a caring majority. This caring majority is the single most powerful weapon there is for creating a safe and caring school environment. There is a way to do this, and as a parent, you may be the first impetus for change. *Bully-Proofing Your School* is a comprehensive guide available to both elementary and middle schools. You can be the one to spearhead change at your child's school. How you approach the school and let them know that there is a way to stop bullying will be important in whether you are heard or just pushed aside as another "overprotective parent."

There are many ways for you to approach your child's school:

1. Talk to your child's teacher and ask if he or she would like to work with you to form a parent-school partnership to explore ways to stop bullying.

2. Obtain a copy of *Bully-Proofing Your School* and share it with your child's school.

3. Talk to other parents. Generate interest and support.

4. Join the Parent Teacher Student Organization and generate interest and support from them.

5. Make an appointment with the school principal. Express your concern without criticizing. Tell the principal that you would like to work together to create a safer school environment not only for your child but for others as well.

Parents are a shaping force within a school. Each classroom, on the average, has two children, at least, who are the victims of a bully. There are other concerned parents. You will not be alone if you make the effort to find them and involve them.

Do's and don'ts to remember

DO	DON'T
Share the problem with the teacher first, then work together to decide how to approach the larger school community.	Go to the parents of the bully.
Explore resources and inform the school of programs for dealing with the problem.	Just complain and demand.
Offer yourself as an ally in solving the problem.	Threaten, hire an attorney, or begin litigation.
Discuss how to make the school safe for all—physically, socially, and psychologically.	Accuse the school of not being safe, as they will become defensive.

Assessing Whether to Change Schools

Consider the following factors when deciding whether to place your child in a different school. In spite of the best efforts of school administrators to change the school environment, your child has been targeted as a victim for such a long period of time that he or she cannot undo or escape being identified as a scapegoat. Some children are so frozen with fear they cannot find the strength to reach out to the caring majority or to stand up for themselves. They have a protective shield and can use it at home, but when the school bully approaches, they are terrified and frozen with fear.

The school administrators have been unresponsive or resistive to your efforts as a parent to bring in a preventative program. They tell you it will be put on the agenda for next year. In the meantime, your child is suffering on a daily basis.

The bullying has escalated to a dangerous level. The cruelty is so intense that your child is avoiding school, feeling very anxious, or physically sick.

Assessing the School's Bully/Victim Climate

When any one of these levels has been reached, it is time to consider a change of schools. As you look for a new school placement, keep these following factors in mind. They will help you find a better fit for your child. If there is no possibility of changing schools within your district, you may want to consider a charter school, private school, or moving to find a kinder school environment. These are extreme measures and only suggested if the bullying is pervasive, lethal, and your child is seriously distressed. If bullying is that extreme at school, changes are it has carried over into the neighborhood as well.

1. A small setting is not always safer.

Many parents assume that a smaller school will provide more protection. There will be a greater staff-to-student ratio, and therefore, they assume that more eyes will be watching. Although this may be the case, watching alone does not stop bullying. A small school may create a "fishbowl" environment where everyone knows what everyone else is doing. There will be fewer children for your child to play with. Avoiding a bully can be more difficult in a small school than in a larger one. There is typically less diversity. If your child is different in some respect, be it a talent, skill, stature, or overall appearance, finding a friend who is similar will be easier in a larger school. Do not automatically assume that small is better. This is not always the case.

2. Observe whether there are helpful adults among the school staff.

Go to the school during recess, lunch, or playtime and watch how children interact together. A bullying incident tends to happen every seven minutes on the average school playground. Stay long enough to see one. Watch carefully for what happens. Is there a staff member nearby? How does that individual intervene? Is there a sense of safety or a feeling of little or no protection?

3. Observe how the children play and interact together during unstructured times.

Do they form groups that exclude others? Do you see small groups of children playing away from the others? Do there appear to be cliques of girls standing about and gossiping? Look around to see if there is a single child standing alone. Pay attention to that child and see whether any of the other children invite him or her to play. Does an adult attempt to intervene or do the adults stand on the sidelines and just watch during playtime? Look for a child who is not as physically active as the others. What is he or she doing? Is there play equipment or games for those children who do not enjoy running, climbing, or organized sports?

4. Ask school administrators whether bullying occurs in the school.

Be suspicious if the school denies such a problem. Most every school, private or public, rural or urban, has problems with bullying. Denying that such problems exist is not a helpful policy. Admitting that some children do bully and explaining that there is an action plan or policy is a more desired response.

5. Watch to see if the teachers and staff reinforce positive behavior.

Look around and observe whether any child makes a thoughtful gesture to another child. Is there an offer to share, to help pick up a spilled backpack, to lend an eraser, or to welcome another into a group? If so, does a teacher or staff member notice and praise the child?

Know your child's strengths and weaknesses.

If you are considering a change of schools, you probably have an overreactive or underreactive child. Remember that your goal is to move your child toward the middle. Do you see the school environment as one that will help shape your child in the desired direction? Changing schools can make a profound difference in the life of a victimized child. It is a new chance, and many badly victimized children have found a new Identity upon changing schools. Remember to select the school based on your child's needs, not on where the others in the neighborhood go or one you feel is most prestigious or rigorous. A victimized child needs a safe environment over and above academics. Children cannot learn when they are afraid. Learning can be made up in time; low self-esteem may be a life-long struggle.

CHAPTER NINE

CHOOSING SPORTS AND RECREATIONAL PROGRAMS

Parents hope that participating in sports will build sportsmanship, skills, and friends. Some of you will watch as your child excels with bursts of joy and excitement. Others will feel anger or sadness as your child sits on the sidelines and rarely plays, or worse yet, suffers humiliation by a coach or teammate.

Sports have a culture of their own. Competition is part of the game. Power and size are often important parts of winning. Unfortunately, winning can sometimes become more important than sportsmanship. Rivalry with other teams can become intense. Ethnic differences may get highlighted to an undesirable extent, and parents often extend their own unfulfilled dreams to their children.

Some children withstand these issues. Those who do are likely to be physically suited to the sport and mature enough to handle the pressure to succeed. For the child who lacks physical stature, ability, and/or emotional maturity, team sports can be brutally humiliating. Seventy percent of all children drop out of organized sports between ages 8 to 13.

Assessing Whether Your Child Is Suited to Team Sports

Parents rarely think about the climate of a sports team or recreational activity until a difficulty arises. Most select a sport because it is high profile in their culture, it has significance to the parent, it is held at a convenient time or place, or the child's best friend is participating in it. Rarely do parents think about their child's skill and maturity, or watch to see the level of competitiveness.

Consider the following three areas before enrolling your child in a sport.

Assess your child for:

- ◆ Interest level
- ◆ Skill
- ◆ Capacity to handle competition
- ◆ Underreactive versus overreactive style
- ◆ Stamina
- ◆ Emotional maturity

Observe the style of the coach:

- ◆ Does everyone play or only the stars?
- ◆ Is there a lot of yelling?
- ◆ Is there demeaning of players?
- ◆ How is losing handled?
- ◆ How is winning handled?
- ◆ Is instruction at a level the children can understand?
- ◆ Do the children demean the coach?

Watch the children on the team:

- ◆ Do they motivate each other with encouragement?
- ◆ How do they handle winning and losing?
- ◆ How do they handle a child who does not play as well as the others?
- ◆ What is the degree of competitiveness?
- ◆ Is everyone included?

Now consider, as a parent, what you want your child to gain from participation. Think back for a moment on your experiences of success as well as your experiences of disappointment, failure, or humiliation. Are you possibly encouraging your child to fulfill **your** dreams—either the ones at which you succeeded or the ones you wish you had?

Think about your child now:

- Is your child more suited to a team sport or an individual sport?
- Is your child more suited to a competitive sport or a recreational one?
- Who has the primary interest in the sport—you or your child?

Matching Your Child to a Sport

The child who will succeed at team sports has the following characteristics:

- High energy
- Stamina
- Coordination
- High pain threshold
- Competitiveness
- Above average size, strength, or agility
- Good frustration tolerance
- Maturity
- Capacity to control anger
- Interpersonal skills
- Capacity to work with others in a group

If your child has these traits, he or she will probably be successful at almost any team sport. If, however, your child has a deficit in skill or size, give serious consideration to skipping the mainstream sports. Look at areas such as track and field, skiing, fencing, and so on. These take skill but with short bursts of focused attention. Size is not a serious part of success and some immaturity can be tolerated.

If your child has a deficit in social maturity, he or she is likely to frustrate quickly, to withdraw, to have temper outbursts, or to not be able to sustain attention. Look at individual sports such as karate, golf, bicycling, swimming, or one-on-one sports such as tennis, racquetball, wrestling, or boxing.

Every child needs a recreational outlet. As a parent, help guide your child into one that will provide success and fun. High-glory sports are not the only ones out there.

What You Can Do If Your Child Is Being Victimized

Think through this practice scenario.

> Your daughter, Maggie, is on the girl's soccer team. They have just resumed play after halftime. Maggie gets the ball and runs it all the way down the field and into the goal. All of the others on her team are yelling her name and chasing after her. Maggie throws up her arms triumphantly after kicking the ball in. Her team boos and boos. Suddenly in horror, Maggie realizes that she ran the wrong direction and scored a goal for the other team.
>
> The rest of the soccer season, Maggie is reminded of her mistake through humiliating comments. Any time she is put in to play, the other girls tease and put her down, saying things like, "Why don't you go play for the other team since that's what you're best at?" or "Do you know your directions yet?" Eventually, Maggie doesn't want to be on the team any longer. She begs you to let her quit.

As a parent, you can:

1. Talk to the coach about creating a climate where bullying is not tolerated and failures are handled with the understanding that all individuals have shortcomings. Publicly ridiculing others should not be acceptable behavior on the team.

2. Let the coach know that you are aware of Maggie's limitations but would like to see her finish the season. Ask if you can work together to accomplish this without public humiliation. Suggest that Maggie go in at less important times in the game or ask about a job for her such as scorekeeping or performing some other important function on the team. Ask the coach to encourage the players to help Maggie improve.

3. Help Maggie build a protective shield. Link her up to at least one other friend on the team. Practice responses to use when she is teased or ridiculed.

4. Work with Maggie to accept her tendency to be impulsive and to go into action before she thinks. Talk about owning shortcomings and accepting them as real but as something to be worked on: "I know I cost us that game—I'm trying to improve. Thanks for letting me have another chance."

What You Can Do as a Parent If Your Child Is Acting Like a Bully

Think through this practice scenario.

> Antoine is the best player on the team. Antoine knows it and he belittles others. To him, everyone else is a slacker. Rarely does the team have enough players at a game to allow the coach to bench a misbehaving player; therefore, Antoine stays in the game. His heroics win the game and his behavior toward his teammates goes unmentioned and undisciplined.

As a parent, you can:

1. Point out to Antoine that there is more to a sports team than just athletic skill. Working together as a team is as important, if not more so. Let him know that he is a talented athlete but he won't go far unless he masters getting along with others on his team.

2. Help Antoine build better interpersonal skills. Let him know that, of course, less skilled players can be frustrating and it would be great if everyone were as capable as he is. Suggest kinder ways to let another player know of his weaknesses such as, "Good try. Lean in a little more next time and you'll have it."

3. Build Antoine's need for power and attention into a leadership role. Talk to the coach about using Antoine to work with others in a positive way.

What You Can Do as a Parent If Your Child Ignores a Victim

Think through this practice scenario.

> Niki, who is a good player, regularly puts down Tosha and Serena. She is downright cruel in her verbal assaults. Eventually Niki is successful in getting two other players to join her in verbally abusing Tosha and Serena. When Niki misses a game, there is much better sportsmanship and team cohesion, yet the players always worry that they need Niki in order to win.

As a parent, you can:

1. Express your own feelings about watching Niki verbally abuse the other two girls. State how it made you feel inside. Ask your child how she felt. Talk together about the guilt most people feel when observing another person being abused. Explain that it is normal and healthy to feel sad and guilty. Having feelings for another person is called empathy and that is a good thing to have.

2. Ask if she has ever considered doing or saying something. Find out what stops her.

3. Look over the list of ideas at the end of Chapter 11. Discuss together what level of risk your daughter might be comfortable trying. Offer your help in practicing the ideas or even trying one out.

Character-Building Through Sports

Sports provide some rich moments for talking with your son or daughter about values. Issues will arise such as: being included or left out, what is a team, how important is winning, and what matters more—the team or the individual? If you spend time at games, you will see these things. Mention them. Listen to your child's view of the situation. Help your child see all sides of the situation. These are teachable moments—make use of them. A teachable moment is an opportunity to promote growth through discussion. It may occur when your child has shown selfishness, immaturity, poor judgment, or unkindness. Rather than just disciplining and lecturing, take the opportunity to build insight, self-awareness, and empathy. Explore healthier ways of problem-solving and coping.

A child asking to quit is a teachable moment. Dropping out without talking about the problem is not a good idea. Changing direction, however, when a situation is harmful and a good effort has been made is a good idea. Take time, therefore, to talk. Discuss what your child does not like. Decide on a plan. If your child is interested in continuing to try, help with putting the plan into action. If, on the other hand, your child decides to quit, go together to the coach and share the reason for the decision.

Remember that participation in sports and activities is meant to be fun. If your child is miserable, go back and assess the three areas listed at the beginning of this chapter. Find an activity that matches your child's abilities and desires.

CHAPTER TEN

PEER INFLUENCES: FRIENDS OR ENEMIES?

Children's friends can also be their enemies. It is not always easy to tell when the boundary has been crossed. One simple rule is that a friendship has evolved into bullying when one of the children is taking far more than he or she is giving. Yet, some children enjoy and benefit from bossy or take-charge friends. What, then, can help a parent to know when a friendship has turned toward a bully/victim relationship?

Recall that bullying occurs when there is no benefit to the victim. Bullying is a one-sided relationship in which the victim is exploited and used.

What Can Parents Do?

Parents may not be able to directly influence the friends their children select to be with at school or in activities, but they can listen, talk about their concerns, and build good judgment. Friendships change over time and across situations. Children may need guidance to understand that friendship is a give-and-take relationship. Repeated mistreatment is not "friendship." Children often need help in recognizing this, defining the limits, working toward change, and even ending a relationship if improvement is not possible. Evaluating the friendship along the following five dimensions can provide a more complete picture for deciding these things:

1. There is repeated maltreatment over time and across varying situations.

2. There is no mutuality.

3. There is little or no empathy, responsiveness, or willingness to problem-solve.

4. There is an element of cruelty—physically or psychologically.

5. The positive private relationship changes to one of maltreatment when peers are present.

If only one or possibly two of these dimensions are present, you may want to encourage your child to work toward improvement in these areas only. If, on the other hand, many of these dimensions are present, the friendship may not be a friendship at all but a bully/victim relationship.

Let's look individually at each area and how to evaluate it.

1.   There is repeated maltreatment over time and situations.

Some children are forced into social settings that are small and in which they are not comfortable. These children have no choice in selecting friends. They are "stuck" in a small environment of peers, be that at school, on the bus, in the neighborhood, at church, or in an activity group. They are essentially held captive. They don't have the choice to walk away and find another group of peers to join.

Negativity in small settings often starts with ostracism—being picked on for being different and being pushed outside of a group by established cliques. Children want to be included socially. One child can be singled out to be excluded, and all of the other children become invested in keeping this child in the underdog role. Changing roles is very difficult once a child has been placed at the bottom of the social-acceptance ladder. This situation often starts with just one child making a cruel remark. This gets the ball rolling and others quickly join in order to affirm their own status in the peer group. As these children don't want to lose their position, they actively join in bullying the victim. Others may remain passive, looking on but allowing the mistreatment to occur. Over time the situation can escalate into one of extreme hurtfulness and viciousness.

> Ryan, who had friends, earned high grades, and excelled at athletics at his previous school, moved during his fifth-grade year to a small private school in a new city. Quickly, he found himself excluded from the small peer group of boys. During a school party, the ringleader of the boys mobilized the others to agree to all get up and leave when Ryan came to sit down at their table. Just as planned, the minute Ryan came to the table, all the others got up and left him on cue from the bully ringleader. The sting of humiliation was enormous for Ryan. Even his little sister, who witnessed what happened, came over and asked what was going on.

Group rejection, such as happened to Ryan, can become almost mob-like. When asked, the other children will justify joining in the cruelty by saying that everyone else does it and that makes it okay. Wanting to be accepted by the group is a powerful influence for many children.

2. There is no mutuality.

Remember that in the give-and-take of friendship, there can be periods of neediness in which one child gives more and the other needs more. Ups and downs are normal, but there must be something in the history of the relationship that promises the give-and-take will be restored in the future. Otherwise, the relationship becomes one-sided.

Watch, for example, how your child and a friend play a game together. Does one child always take the favorite color token first, or announce who will be the "banker," or change the rules to assure winning? If your child says this feels unfair, does the other child get even more strong willed or do they work together to find a fair solution?

Notice if a friend constantly asks to borrow things from your child. Are valued things taken home by the other and never returned? When you, as a parent, set limits on borrowing, is the limit respected and the loaned object returned? Or, on the other hand, is an excuse always made for why the loaned object cannot be found or returned?

Find out if such a friend is having a particularly difficult time at home. Neediness can manifest itself from time to time when life is difficult. For example, two nine-year-old girls found their friendship being strained when one of the girls repeatedly took favorite things from her friend, whined endlessly, and bragged constantly about her own accomplishments. When the victimized girl came to realize that her friend's family was having serious problems emotionally and financially, she was able to be more understanding and patient. She also learned to set limits and ask for more fairness in the friendship. Over time, the "bully" friend began to feel better and to have more capacity to give back. Six months later, when the victimized child had to face a scary situation alone, her friend offered to go out of her way to accompany her to make it easier. There was, in time, the giving back that true friendship is about.

3.   There is no empathy, responsiveness, or problem solving.

Problem-solving is learned gradually in the middle years of childhood. Not until age eight or nine do most children recognize the concept of "fairness" and how to talk through difficulties. To have the capacity to problem-solve, a child must first be able to recognize another child's needs. This involves awareness of others, the capacity to listen and process feelings, and some appreciation that each person is unique in what hurts feelings. A self-serving child is one who always places his or her needs above all other considerations. Even if your child and his or her friend cannot problem-solve together, watch to see if one or both can accept a fair solution when you offer it. If fairness is repeatedly turned down and only a self-serving outcome is acceptable, then the friendship has turned toward becoming a bully/victim relationship.

> Two boys, Mark and Matt, were playing together in the family room at Mark's house. Matt found some money under a couch cushion. He quickly announced that he planned to keep the money and that "next time either of us finds money, you'll get it." Of course, the odds that there would be a "next time" to find money were slim. When Mark's mother attempted to help the boys problem-solve by suggesting that a fairer approach would be to share the money both this time and "next time," Matt absolutely rejected this idea. As he left for home with the money in hand, Matt evidenced little remorse or concern for how his friend might be feeling or for the fact that the money had most likely been lost by someone from Mark's home. This type of interactional style, with no willingness to problem-solve, does not bode well for the future of a relationship. In fact, the friendship

between Mark and Matt continued for many years after the money episode. Matt repeatedly came to Mark for favors. The favors grew larger and more serious as time went by. The requested favors were for loans of larger and larger amounts of money or to be "put up" for months at a time. Ultimately, Mark realized that what he had believed to be a friendship was more honestly characterized as a exploitative relationship. Mark ended it at that point.

4. There is an element of cruelty.

Some children are clueless and truly lack any awareness of how their negative behavior feels to others. This may be due to deprivation in learning this awareness, but help is available and effective in improving children's social skills. Other children in this category actually get pleasure out of hurting others. They may be hard-core, angry children who don't want help and will not accept it. This type of child is not one you can turn into a friend by any means. These children are determined to win and they will become more vicious in order to "get even." Teach your child to stay away from these children. They will never become friends.

> Luis, an adult today, described such a classmate during his childhood years. In spite of appearing to be a strong and competent adult male, Luis trembled as he recalled the following episode of leaving school one day. While walking home, Luis and some friends were approached by Roy, who started to heckle them. Luis had his hockey skates slung over his shoulders as he walked along. At first, the group ignored Roy; nevertheless Roy tagged along calling them names and threatening them. Finally Luis told him to "take a hike," and Roy grabbed the hockey skates and slammed the blade into Luis' head. Today Luis has an ugly scar where he received stitches from his eyebrow to his scalp. Roy laughed and jeered, pleased with his feat and not at all alarmed at the serious injury he had inflicted. A few days later, Luis, with his head still bandaged, opened his locker to find a dead cat hanging from the coathook. Roy casually passed by in the hall and told him that was his warning for "next time."

Children such as Roy are frightening. They will hurt others and many grow up to be criminals who feel pleasure in watching others suffer. This is way beyond what any children should be handling. Authority figures must be brought in to help with situations this serious and intense. No child, whether victim or bystander, has the capacity to cope with this level of cruelty.

5. The relationship changes to one of maltreatment when peers are present.

Some friendships seem to change dramatically when other children are present. Your child may play successfully with a peer one-on-one, only to find that he or she is treated very differently in the presence of peers. These are "underground friendships" because they exist away from the eyes of the rest of the world. As a parent, you need to understand these relationships before planning what to do. Typically, the child who changes colors does it to find acceptance in the peer group. He or she is unlikely to be the ringleader of the bullying behavior; rather, this child is a "lieutenant." A lieutenant is a child who plays by the rules the bully sets when the bully is present, but is more of his or her own person when alone.

These situations cause tremendous hurt and confusion to your child who will question why someone is a friend when alone and then "turn coat" when with others. Since you can guess that the child is not the bully, your first job as a parent is to figure out who the bully is and who the followers or lieutenants are. The lieutenants can most likely be influenced to change their behavior. An outside adult who is present during these peer interactions will need to help in defusing the bully's power and reshaping the climate of the peer play. The first step is to occupy the bully in another activity. If the behavior of the lieutenants changes when the bully is gone from the play group, it becomes obvious who is shaping the behavior. If the lieutenants accept the victimized child as a playmate when the bully is away, then new bonds of friendship can form and things will change by themselves as time goes by. The bully may or may not be able to be reintroduced into the play group.

What Else Can Parents Do?

The following list gives a concise summary of what you can do to help your child.

1. Evaluate the friendship with your child along the five dimensions. Gently advise your child to get out of the friendship if too many dimensions are worrisome.

2. Balance the odds for your child by building resiliency and social skills.

3. Mobilize the community to change the climate and make it safer for all.

4. Contact an authority figure who will work with you in a confidential manner if you believe your child is being bullied by a seriously cruel and sadistic child.

5. Do not contact the parents of the bully on your own. Parents of bullies will defend their own bully and the problem usually gets worse, not better. Use your connections in the community to bring about change by mobilizing other children and adults.

6. Talk with your child to identify who the helpful adults are. Not all adults are helpful. Children constantly report that they went to a person whose title or position indicated the adult would help only to be told, "You are old enough to solve your own problems." Ask your child, "Who do you think would help you?" Let your child name some people. You may be surprised at your child's awareness and resourcefulness.

7. Remember that children drift in and out of friendships. Do not attempt to repair some friendships or encourage friends who have lost their appeal. Some change is inevitable as different ages bring new interests, activities, and possibilities for friendship. Few children keep their childhood friends for life.

CHAPTER ELEVEN

CREATING A PLAN FOR THE RESISTIVE CHILD

Teaching your child to handle bully/victim problems is giving him or her skills for life. The ideas will be useful in many other difficult situations. You cannot be there at every moment. Involve your children in solving their own struggles. Teach them to think and trust that they can make their own good judgment calls.

Throughout the book, ideas have been presented for managing bullies. Some children, however, complain but resist help. They want you to do it for them. You may be tempted, but do not give in. A "Bully Intervention Plan" must involve your child in solving his or her problem. If you do it, nothing will be learned or mastered. Be cautious. Do not jump in too quickly with a solution. Allow your child to struggle a bit to create ideas. Make time for talking and problem-solving together. There are three steps in building a plan:

1. Assess the Problem

2. Problem Solve Together

3. Develop a Plan

Now, think for a moment about your child's style. As eager as most children are for relief from bullies, they typically want the adults to figure out a plan and take care of the problem for them. Talking about the bully/victim situation and creating a plan is not easy. Children have an array of avoidance styles they use. Some of these are:

- Whining about it but not solving it. "You talk to him, Dad."
- Refusing to talk. "Butt out, Mom."
- Blaming. "It's the other guy's fault."
- Giving up. "There's nothing anyone can do that will help."

These are the emotional roadblocks children may put up. These tactics will distract you, convince you that you must either do it for them, that the problem is too big to solve, or your child doesn't need your help. It is difficult not to get snagged by the hooks and then get taken in by your child's difficulty in facing a troublesome issue. You don't need to let that happen. Don't give in to helplessness.

There are five areas you will want to explore and create answers to as part of the dialogue and problem-solving discussion you have with your child. Think of it as an interview. Don't give the answers. If you were interviewing someone for a job, you wouldn't answer the questions for that person. If you did, you would never learn what the person was like and whether he or she had the skills for the job. This is precisely what you want to know about your own child. How was the problem experienced—did it create fear, anger, anxiety, sadness? Does he or she have appropriate ideas, skills, and solutions for handling it, or do some need to be suggested or created?

Consider these five questions. Be as objective as you can.

1. What happened?
2. How did you feel when this happened?
3. What can you do about it?
4. What is the risk in doing this?
5. If this worked, what would be different?

Overcoming Styles of Resistance

Let's look now at the different styles children have when a parent attempts to get a dialogue started.

For the Reluctant Whiner
(The child who whines about the problem)

1. Ask your child to list all of the barriers that get in the way.

   ◆ Write them down. There may be as many as ten or more.

   ◆ Don't react emotionally or say how silly certain complaints are; just listen and write.

   ◆ Don't comment on your child's sense of helplessness.

2. Ask your child to put a star by the two he or she might be able to do something about.

3. Create a plan for these two areas (ignore the others for now).

Children who adopt this style truly feel overwhelmed with emotion and cannot move from the state of experiencing the feeling to creating a solution. They quickly flood with feelings, focus only on their own internal state, and panic at the thought that they might have to assert themselves to solve the problem. Often they have had others who did it for them in the past. They have learned to feel helpless and dependent rather than powerful and resourceful. No matter how small the effort they are willing to make, they will gain confidence from doing something rather than doing nothing.

Even if your child's plan is minuscule and you know it is not going to really solve the whole problem, encourage him or her and offer praise for having made a valiant effort. Encourage your child to use a friend, the peer group, or another helpful adult. If parents implement all of the aspects of the intervention plan, the child will not build confidence and strength. These children will benefit by exerting themselves to struggle to the extent that they are capable.

For the Silent Sufferer
(The child who won't communicate)

1. Try saying, "I heard you had a rough day yesterday. When you want to talk about it, let me know," or "I have some new ideas

about the problem you had the other day. Let me know when you have time to hear them."

2. Walk away.

Eventually these children will come to talk about the problem, but on their own timetable, not on yours. Walking away gives them power in that you have respected what they say they want. Acknowledging that a problem did happen also lets them know that you are not going to ignore or deny difficulties. Some of these children adopt this style to gain power through withholding. They fear that talking with someone will mean that person will take control of their lives. Helplessness terrifies them. Others use this style because they honestly cannot communicate about feelings—their own or others. Refusing to communicate protects their secret and doesn't reveal their vulnerabilities or lack of skill and ability to communicate.

For the Externalizer
(The child who blames someone else)

1. Let your child know that you know what happened.

2. Listen to the entire description of the experience from your child's perspective without interruption. Then calmly ask, "What was your part?"

3. Without passing judgment, point out that there may be long-range consequences to be experienced even if it was the other child's fault.

4. Say, "I may not have the right answer, but I'd be happy to talk about it so you don't find yourself in trouble later."

5. Label any feelings that are shared with an empathic response, such as, "Looks like you are really struggling."

6. Be creative and start a dialogue about possible solutions and intervention plans. Try to suggest some that are humorous, fun, or engaging rather than power positions. Support any healthy intervention ideas your child comes up with.

Many of these children avoid exposing themselves and their feelings at all costs. Some are truly lacking in insight. They most sincerely see the onset of all problems as something done **to** them. This is a risky position to take in life because it eliminates the necessity for dialoguing and problem-solving. Believing that others are always at fault takes away personal responsibility for problem-solving. Many of these are the children who get into serious trouble later in life in relationships and in jobs. They cannot get along with people because they cannot own their own part in creating difficult social situations. It is tempting to want to insist that these children see their own part in creating a problem and to want to punish them to teach them a lesson. Don't do either because it only drives in deeper the sense of alienation and estrangement that they feel. The key to solving the problem is in building and modeling a relationship, establishing trust, and hoping that these children will eventually experience intimacy and the rewards that come with a relationship. Your initial goal must be a simple one—just to build communication, shared feelings, and a plan for solving a problem in a way that doesn't mean being cruel to another person.

There is another type of child who falls into this category. These children are the "lieutenants." They blame others, usually the bully but possibly also the victim, while often failing to recognize that they too have a choice in whether to follow the lead of the bully. The bully is important to them in the power structure. By aligning with this person, the lieutenant remains safe. What he or she is sacrificing, however, is a sense of personal choice. The cost of safety is aligning with a poor model—a model who is teaching how to use put-downs, cruelty, and intimidation to get what he or she wants from others. A healthier choice may be to gain the skills to dialogue with others, to be respected by others, and to achieve power through strength of character. For these children, the first step is to build self-awareness. The ultimate goal is one of creating individual solutions separate from those created by the bully. Learning not to follow the crowd, but to think for oneself, is the behavior to shape. The more you can engage your child in creative problem-solving with you, the better off he or she will be in identifying better choices.

For the Child Beyond Hope
(The child who believes there is nothing anyone can do)

1. Listen carefully for the following as your child talks about the bully/victim situation. Does he or she exhibit:
   - a very high degree of fear
   - a strong sense of helplessness and hopelessness
   - a sense that no one can possibly help or change the situation
   - sadness

♦ a loss of interest in school

♦ a sense of no friends

2. If your child is feeling some of the above, be compassionate and communicate that there is hope.

3. Reassure your child that when bully/victim problems get this out of hand, it takes a team approach to solve them.

4. Let your child know that you are going to work with him or her every step of the way to think through a comprehensive plan. Creating such a plan might involve a number of steps that will need to be worked through together and possibly with others. For example, it may involve:

♦ approaching the right person at the school and asking for help in changing the climate of the school

♦ finding some friends to feel safe with

♦ finding a counselor to help with the feelings of sadness

♦ joining a group to work on social skills

These children are often so defeated and hopeless about the bully problems that they believe no help is possible. They suffer silently and live each day at school with a great deal of fear. School or the activity in which the bullying occurs is no longer fun or of any interest to them. The social environment has become so miserable that enjoyment is no longer possible. There is a difference between hopeless children and whiny children. Hopeless children may not even have the energy to convey a long list of complaints. They often have given up all hope that change is possible. Attempting to encourage them to assert themselves or stand up for their rights will be futile because they don't have the energy or self-confidence to muster the effort.

It is critically important that you convey a sense of hope to your child and that you demonstrate interventions on his or her behalf. Until some margin of safety is felt at school, some friends found, and better feelings built, your child will not be capable of learning, much less using the protective and coping skills presented in earlier chapters. Gradually, you and a counselor can introduce these.

If the sense of sadness does not begin to change as the environment improves, you may need to consider a stronger course of action. Finding a competent child mental health professional, preferably one familiar with bully/victim problems, may truly be a favor to this child. This extent of sadness should not be part of childhood, and outside help can often support you as a parent in relieving these feelings for your child. A change of schools is also a possibility to consider. Some children have been so severely bullied that the image of being the victim just cannot be changed in their current school environment. This is especially true in small settings where there is little choice in finding new friends and everyone "lives in a fishbowl," knowing all about each other. A larger school with more diversity can allow more choices for friends, activities, and safety.

Creating a Plan

Your final goal as a parent is to work jointly with your child to create an intervention plan. By now, if you have read through the earlier chapters, you have the skills you need to know your child, to know yourself, and to address the important issues. Most important, do not do it alone—work as a team with your child to create a plan.

CHAPTER TWELVE

SKILLS FOR LIFE

Most children are bystanders. They are not victims. They are not bullies. These children, however, suffer too. They know what is happening and who is getting bullied, and later in life they often report feeling guilty for not doing anything to help the victim or for joining in when they knew it was wrong.

Friends may entice your child into bullying others. It takes courage to stand up for another child when there is social pressure to join in. You can explore with your child how much he or she can risk in order to help. Some children cannot take a stand alone. It feels too frightening and threatening, but they may be able to join in if another child goes first and sets the trend.

Learning to Take Risks

There are a number of ways to help. Some carry more risk than others. Look over Table 7 and consider what fits your child's style and the situations he or she may observe. Not every idea is for every child. Remember, however, that doing something is better than doing nothing. Sometimes only one child has the courage to do what is fair, and then, surprisingly, others join in. These strategies or ideas carry different levels of risk. Some are safe and comfortable for most children, whereas others require extraordinary courage and leadership skill. Do not push your child into a position or risk he or she is not ready to take. Find the right one. Courage and character strength build slowly over time and across many situations.

Look again at Table 7. Five different strategies are identified, and each has a level of risk that ranges from low to high. Most children are capable of low risk. Many children just don't think of or consider these ideas. Share them with your child and practice how he or she might use them in real-life situations.

TABLE 7   Levels of Risk

Strategies of Intervention	LOW - - - - - - - - - - - - - - - - - - HIGH		
Not Joining In	Walk away.	Stay but do not participate.	Declare your nonparticipation.
Getting Adult Help	Get help anonymously.	Identify who the helpful adults are and get one of them.	Announce loudly your intention to get adult help; then do it.
Mobilizing Peer Group	Identify a peer leader and offer to join in standing up to the bully.	Identify others who are capable of mobilizing peers in defense of the victim and recruit them to the cause.	Be a leader in recruiting others to join in standing up to the bully.
Taking an Individual Stand	Go over to the victim and lead him or her away from the situation.	Say, "Leave him alone."	Say, "We don't treat people like that at our school."
Befriending the Victim	Privately empathize with the victim by saying, "That was unfair or cruel."	Go over and stand with the victim or invite him or her to join you in doing something else.	Stand with the victim and publicly announce the "unfair" behavior of the bully.

Children who have the guts to stand up to the bully, at some level of risk, build their own character in the process of helping someone else. Often they are noticed by other children and adults and admired and recognized for their willingness to take some risk on behalf of another person. A wonderful story appeared in many newspapers not long ago about a small group of children who set the tone for an entire class and eventually for many others around the nation. One boy in a classroom had lost his hair due to chemotherapy. He was being teased and made fun of for something that obviously was tragic. A number of other boys in his class decided to shave their hair off as a show of strength and joining in. A few days later the rest of the boys did the same. When the teacher saw the courage the students had demonstrated, he joined in as well. Needless to say, the bullying stopped and a great deal of admiration was garnered by the entire class.

RESOURCE GUIDE FOR PARENTS AND CHILDREN

Books for Parents

Conari Press (eds.). (1994). *Kids' random acts of kindness*. Emeryville, CA: Conari Press.

This book celebrates the joy of connecting with another person, while encouraging this value in children. Children from around the world flooded the editors of Conari Press with their refreshingly tender stories. The selections published here remind us all of the vital and joyful role that kindness can play in our lives.

Diamond, J. (1996). Friendship Note Paper. Great Eye deas Press, P.O. Box 101015, Denver, CO 80250.

A step-by-step guide for use with a group of children as a cooperative and fund-raising endeavor. Teaches the concepts of social cooperation and the value of a friend in the process.

Dosic, W. (1995). *Golden Rules*. San Francisco: HarperCollins.

A simple guide to ten basic values taught through stories, anecdotes, proverbs, and real life examples.

Eyre, L. & Eyre, R. (1993). *Teaching your children values*. New York: Simon & Schuster.

Practical, fun family activities for developing values in children such as honesty, respect, self-discipline, and others.

Goleman, D. (1995). *Emotional intelligence*. New York: Bantam Books.

A persuasive book on why character development in children is more important than intelligence for success later in life. Practical ways to build these skills in your children are presented.

Huggins, P. (1993a). *Helping kids handle anger* (2nd ed.). Longmont, CO: Sopris West.

Includes lessons designed to enable both primary and intermediate students to acknowledge, accept, and constructively express anger.

Students learn: (1) to use inner speech to inhibit aggressive behavior; (2) to use thinking skills for choosing constructive behavior when angry; (3) appropriate language to express anger; (4) a variety of techniques to release energy after anger arousal; (5) ways to defuse the anger of others; and (6) a model for resolving classroom conflicts. Role-plays and puppets are utilized to encourage active student involvement.

Huggins, P. (1993b). *Teaching friendship skills: Intermediate version.* Longmont, CO: Sopris West.

Contains lessons and supplementary activities. Students identify behaviors in others that attract them and behaviors that alienate them. They examine their own behavior and determine changes they need to make in order to gain friends. They learn how to curb physical and verbal aggression. They discover that the secret to making friends is to make others feel special and practice specific ways to do so. They learn the value of sharing and how to give sincere compliments and apologies. In addition, this version focuses on listening, understanding others' perspectives and feelings, and being honest but kind. It also contains 56 activities designed for a Multiple Intelligences Friendship Center.

Huggins, P. (1993c). *Teaching friendship skills: Primary version.* Longmont, CO: Sopris West.

This version contains all new lessons and supplementary activities. Students identify behaviors in others that attract them and behaviors that alienate them. They examine their own behavior and determine changes they need to make in order to gain friends. They learn how to curb physical and verbal aggression. They discover that the secret to making friends is to make others feel special and practice specific ways to do so. This version provides a comprehensive bibliography of children's books on friendship. Puppets, games, role-plays, kinesthetic activities, and goal setting are used to increase motivation and transfer of training.

Katz, M. (1997). *On playing a poor hand well.* New York: W.W. Norton.

An examination of trauma and adversity in childhood, and how to overcome it and build resilience.

Kellerman, Jonathan. (1999). *Savage Spawn:* Reflections on Violent Children. NY: Ballantine Publishing.

A frank examination by a noted child psychologist of the factors during childhood which contribute to violence in children and adolescents.

McGinnis, E. & Goldstein, A.P. (1984). *Skillstreaming the elementary school child.* Champaign, IL: Research Press.

The program covers 60 specific prosocial skills such as saying thank you, asking for help, apologizing, dealing with anger, responding to teasing, and handling group pressure. Addresses the needs of students who display aggression, immaturity, withdrawal, and other problem behaviors.

Paley, V.G. (1992). *You can't say, you can't play.* Cambridge, MA: Howard University Press.

Details an experimental year in the kindergarten classroom of Vivian Paley, an innovative teacher and educator, who introduces the rule, "You can't say, 'You can't play.' " In other words, no child is allowed to reject or leave out another child who wishes to be included in play. Not only are the voices of the children heard as they adapt to this new order, but those of the older fifth graders observing the process are shared as well.

Rubin, A. (1980). *Children's friendships.* Cambridge, MA: Harvard University Press.

A wonderful book that traces friendships developmentally from the preschool-aged child through adolescence.

Samenow, S. (1989). *Before it's too late: Why some kids get into trouble and what parents can do about it.* New York: Random House.

This book describes the thinking patterns of antisocial children and shows parents how they might inadvertently be facilitating the antisocial behavior. Easy to read and understand, this book is full of good ideas for parents and professionals alike.

Schulman, M. & Mekler, E. (1994). *Bringing up a moral child: A new approach to teaching your child to be kind, just and responsible.* New York: Doubleday.

A variety of ideas for building empathy, fairness, and moral development in children from birth through adolescence.

Seligman, M. (1995). *The optimistic child.* New York: Harper Perennial.

A program for both parents and teachers in identifying the early signs of depression and turning children toward optimism and hope for their future.

Shure, M.B. (1994). *Raising a thinking child: Help your young child learn to resolve conflicts and get along with others.* New York: Holt.

A cognitive approach to building thinking skills in young children. This approach strongly correlates with good problem-solving and social skills later in life.

Trovato, C. (1987). *Teaching kids to care.* Cleveland, OH: Instructor Books.

A guide to understanding and developing a prosocial environment both within the classroom as well as within the home. Specifically focuses on ages 2–6 with special chapters on disabilities and ethnic differences.

Books for Primary Students

Alexander, M. (1981). *Move over, twerp.* New York: Dial Books.

An enchanting story showing the resourcefulness of a young boy who employs humor to solve a bullying problem. The victim is very endearing—a great silent majority book. Currently out of print. Check your library.

Bennett, W. (1995). *The children's book of virtues.* New York: Simon & Schuster.

Fables and folklore that teach the principles of good character. Beautifully illustrated.

Boyd, L. (1991). *Baily the big bully.* New York: Puffin Books.

This story wins by persuasion, showing a bully that it is more fun to be a friend. It is out of print, but worth the trip to the library.

Brown, M. (1990). *Arthur's April fool.* Boston: Little, Brown & Co.

Arthur's April Fool's surprise is almost spoiled by a bully.

Browne, A. (1989). *Willy the wimp.* New York: Knopf.

How to be gentle and kind without being a victim.

Browne, A. (1991). *Willy and Hugh.* New York: Knopf.

How friendship and mutuality can prevent bullying.

Carlson, N. (1983). *Loudmouth George and the sixth grade bully.* New York: Puffin Books.

How George, with the help of his friend Harriet, thwarts an older and larger boy from stealing his lunch. How to support a victimized child through friendship is the theme of this story.

Carlson, N. (1988). *I like me.* New York: Viking.

An appealing little book about taking care of and valuing yourself. This book would be especially helpful for victimized children.

Carlson, N. (1994). *How to lose all your friends.* New York: Viking.

> With humor and colorful illustrations, Carlson shows how unappealing children are who put down others and are poor sports.

Moser, A. (1991). *Don't feed the monster on Tuesday.* Kansas City, MO: Landmark Editions.

> A wonderful book that presents valuable information to children about the importance of self-esteem. Practical approaches are presented that children can use to evaluate and strengthen their sense of self-esteem. A very practical guide to taking small steps toward success. Recommended for grades K–5, and definitely recommended for victimized children.

Naylor, P. (1991). *King of the playground.* New York: Simon & Schuster.

> How one young boy handles a playground bully.

Zolotow, C. (1982). *The quarreling book.* New York: HarperCollins Children's Books.

> A short story about how a quarrel can grow bigger and bigger until it hurts many people. For the youngest elementary children, this book builds an understanding of how aggression can spread unless stopped. A beginning guide to empower the silent majority.

Books for Intermediate Students

Bosch, C. (1988). *Bully on the bus.* Seattle, WA: Parenting Press.

> A terrific book that allows the reader to select from different options of how to handle a bully encountered on the school bus. For example, the victim can decide to fight back or to ask a friend for help by turning to different pages to learn the outcome. Children eventually read all the options, curious to find out which one proves the most effective. Many good ideas are presented for victimized children.

Burnett, Karen (1999). *Simon's hook: A book about teases and put downs.* Roseville, CA: GR Publishing. P.O. Box 1437, Roseville, CA 95678, or www.grandmarose.com.

> When Simon is teased about a bad haircut, Grandma Rose teaches him, through an analogy to fishing, how not to take the bait. A truly terrific story adaptable to any situation involving verbal abuse and teasing.

Cohen-Posey, K. (1995). *How to handle bullies, teasers, and other meanies.* Highland City, FL: Rainbow Books. P.O. Box 430, Highland City, FL 33846-0430.

> Effective techniques for handling insults, teasing, and overall bullying.

Coombs, K. (1991). *Beating bully O'Brien*. New York: Avon Books.

A fifth grade boy is physically assaulted by a girl bully on his way home from school. His dad makes him feel like a sissy for not defending himself, but the boy is a viola player and does not want to hurt his hands. When the bully's older brother attacks the boy, the girl bully intervenes and helps him. He later learns that she gets beaten up at home by her older brother. A good silent majority book, as the main character is very likable.

Estes, E. (1944). *The hundred dresses*. New York: Harcourt Brace Jovanovich.

A Newberry Honor story that will touch hearts: about the humiliation that results from teasing among elementary-aged girls. A good story to empower the silent majority.

Frankel, F. (1996). *Good friends are hard to find*. Los Angeles: Perspective Publishing.

Specific steps for parents and children to follow together for handling problems in friendships.

Kaufman, G. & Raphael, L. (1990). *Stick up for yourself*. Minneapolis, MN: Free Spirit Publishing.

A guide to assertiveness and positive self-esteem. Discusses problems such as making choices, learning about and liking yourself, and solving problems. Recommended for grades 4–8. A wealth of ideas for victimized children.

Romain, T. (1997). *Bullies are a pain in the brain*. Minneapolis, MN: Free Spirit Publishing.

A small book packed with humor and good advice for handling bullies.

Stolz, M. (1963). *The bully of Barkham Street*. New York: HarperCollins Children's Books.

The main character in this story is the bully. He is a sixth grade boy who is the oldest and biggest in his classroom. His family rarely listens to him and often threatens to take away his only friend, his dog.